Animal Tracking:
Learn More About Animals

by Donna Watson

Scott Foresman
is an imprint of

Glenview, Illinois • Boston, Massachusetts • Chandler, Arizona
Upper Saddle River, New Jersey

ISBN 13: 978-0-328-51391-8
ISBN 10: 0-328-51391-1

Getting On Track

People have tracked animals in the wild for thousands of years. In the past, people tracked animals and studied their habits in order to hunt them. More recently, people have tracked wildlife in order to help endangered animals. Wildlife **biologists,** who study living things, follow and watch animals to record and study **data,** or information, about them.

The easiest way for biologists to find animals is to follow their footprints. This works in mud, snow, or wet sand. But what about animals that spend their entire lives in the water or in the air, never touching the ground? Obviously they don't leave footprints! Luckily there are many other ways to find animals.

Can you see the tracks this duck has made?

What if a biologist wants to investigate an animal and can't find any tracks? Biologists are usually able to find other signs that an animal has been nearby. For instance, grizzly bears rub against trees to leave a scent. In the process, they strip bark from the trees and leave behind their fur. Biologists study the stripped bark, scent, and fur to learn more about bears.

Like bears, male white-tailed deer also rub against trees in order to leave a scent. Their antlers leave marks on the trees as they rub up against them. Porcupines eat tree bark, leaving marks near the base of trees. Beavers take down small trees by chewing them down to stumps. They use the trees to build their homes, which are called lodges. The pointed tree stumps, lodges, and dams that beavers build help make a beaver's habitat easy to identify.

The diagram below shows what a typical beaver lodge looks like. Can you see the two entrances that the beavers have made? Biologists can tell many things about beavers by studying their lodges. Because of the lodges they make, beavers are some of the easiest animals to track.

Beavers use small trees to build lodges and dams.

Other Kinds of Tracks

One of the signs used to track animals is **scat,** or animal droppings. Each animal's scat has its own color, size, and shape. **Mammal** scat is the easiest to **classify,** or group.

Scat contains many clues that help biologists track animals. Its location helps tell which animal made it. Scat may also tell when the animal was there as well as what it ate. Wolves and coyotes usually have fur in their scat. Black bears leave piles of scat in thick cords.

Owl pellets may look like scat, but they aren't. Owls swallow their prey whole. However they cannot digest hair, feathers, or bones. Instead of digesting them, they turn them into pellets and cough them up. The pellets are found at the base of trees. Pellets are one sign biologists look for when they are tracking owls.

An owl pellet, which contains the bones, hair, and feathers of its prey

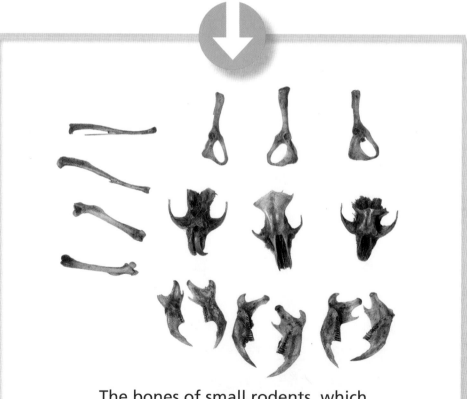

The bones of small rodents, which are one source of food for owls

Tracking with Radio Collars

Radio collars allow biologists to track animals from far away. To place a radio collar around an animal's neck, the tracker uses special medicine, called **tranquilizers,** to make the animal sleepy. Sometimes trackers are lucky enough to find animals that are already **hibernating,** or sleeping. It is much easier to place radio collars on hibernating animals.

Biologists often put radio collars on hibernating bears. First they locate a bear's den. Then they creep into the den and put a collar around the bear's neck while it sleeps.

Radio collars can be used to study elks' movements.

Radio collar on a moose in Gros Morne National Park, Newfoundland, Canada.

This same way of tracking can also be used for observing eagles. Once a collar is placed around an eagle's leg, trackers follow the moving bird to find out where it is nesting and how far it must travel to get food. When tracking smaller birds, biologists attach the radio collar to the bird's back. The collar fits around the bird's wings. Before biologists fit a collar around a bird's leg or back, they make sure that the bird can fly while wearing it.

Radio collars are used to track many kinds of animals. Nowadays there are more modern devices that biologists use to track animals. But radio collars still work quite well.

Tracking with GPS

Another way to track animals is to use a Global Positioning System, also called GPS. A biologist will fit an animal with a GPS collar. The collar sends a signal that is picked up by satellites circling Earth. The satellites use the signals to locate the animal. Then they send the animal's exact location to a computer. The biologist can check on the animal's movement many times during a day. Even better, collars that use GPS can last up to two years!

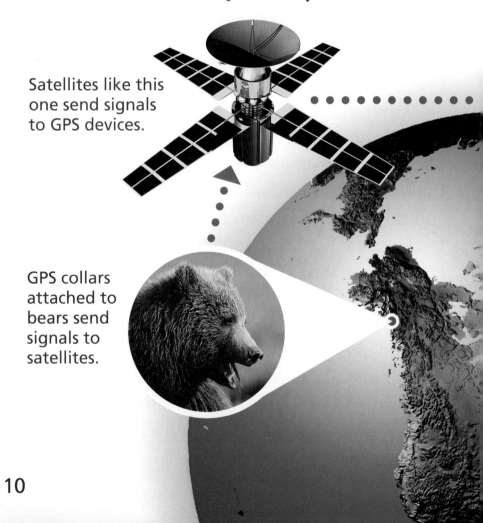

Satellites like this one send signals to GPS devices.

GPS collars attached to bears send signals to satellites.

GPS is an excellent way for biologists to study an animal's travel patterns. It can also be used to take a **measurement** of an animal's hunting range. GPS provides regular, detailed data on an animal's location. However, GPS collars are heavier than radio collars. Also, GPS information shows up only as a dot on a computer screen. Because of that, biologists who use GPS collars don't get to view the animal they are studying.

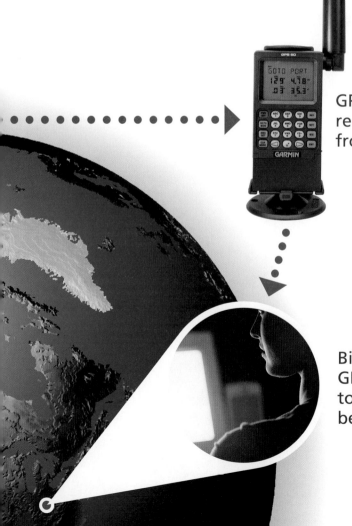

GPS devices receive signals from satellites.

Biologists use GPS signals to track the bears.

Tracking Cranes in Planes

Both radio and GPS collars have been used to help save the whooping crane. Hunting and loss of habitat had reduced the whooping crane population to about twenty birds. In order to save these animals, biologists started raising whooping cranes in captivity. They hoped that it would only take a short period of time to get the young cranes ready for release into the wild.

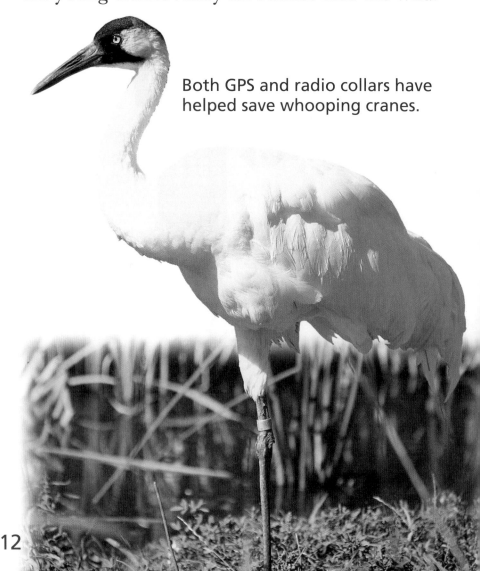

Both GPS and radio collars have helped save whooping cranes.

Sometimes chicks have difficulty migrating.

There was only one problem: The crane chicks did not know that they were supposed to move south, or **migrate,** for the winter. Biologists had to teach the whooping cranes to fly from Wisconsin to Florida. The biologists decided that the best way to do this would be if they dressed up as birds! The whooping cranes had radio and GPS collars placed around their legs. They were trained to follow an airplane flown by pilots wearing crane costumes. As you'll read, this idea ran into difficulties. Overall, though, the experiment was a great success.

From the start, the whooping cranes were able to follow the plane. Their migration took longer than normal because the airplane had to fly low in the sky. That forced the birds to flap their wings more often. The airplane also put the cranes at risk by leading them close to power lines and other dangerous things.

Biologists taught whooping cranes to migrate by flying in planes.

Using the radio collars, biologists were able to find whooping cranes that had been blown off course or become lost. Once the birds arrived safely in Florida, they spent the winter with other whooping cranes. In the spring, they migrated back to Wisconsin on their own, without the help of the plane. The biologists tracked the whooping cranes' flight back to Wisconsin by monitoring their GPS collars.

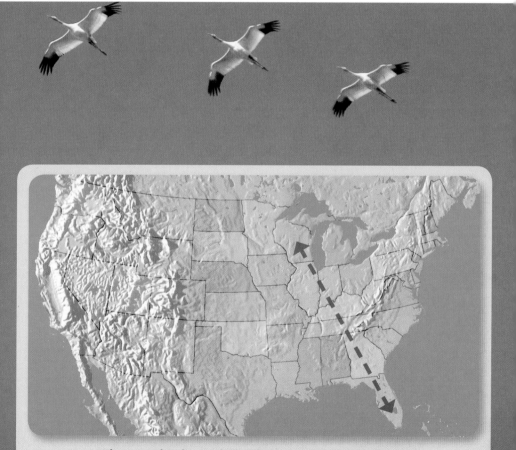

The path the whooping cranes migrated from Wisconsin to Florida and back.

Tracking Blue Whales

Another special type of satellite tracking has been used to study blue whales. These whales usually travel in groups, with two to four whales in each group. Biologists wanted to know where the whales liked to search for food and where they migrated to each year. By using a special crossbow, they were able to attach satellite transmitters to about one hundred whales. The satellite transmitters have provided new information for biologists to record and **analyze,** or examine carefully.

Biologists have learned about blue whales through satellite tracking.

The transmitters that were attached to the blue whales had to work successfully with the largest animals in the world! With smaller animals, biologists have to use other kinds of tracking devices. Microchip transmitters are one such kind of tracking device. They work very well with small animals such as snakes. A biologist will take a microchip transmitter and place it under a snake's skin. The transmitter will not harm the snake at all while it's attached.

Microchip transmitters have helped biologists understand the mating, hunting, and hibernating habits of snakes. Unfortunately, microchip transmitters are expensive. Because of this many scientists cannot afford to use them while they are studying animals.

Microchip transmitters cause other problems. Although they are the safest type of tracking devices, it can be difficult to place them under the skin of the animal being tracked.

Tracking Through Tag-and-Release

Another method of tracking that has been used for fish, amphibians, birds, and mammals is the tag-and-release method. Here's how it works: Biologists catch an animal like a red wolf. They mark it with a special tag. The wolf is then returned to the wild. Biologists try to recapture the wolf later on at a different location.

Tag-and-release is risky. The biologists might not be able to recapture the wolf later on!

Park rangers and biologists attach a radio collar to a red wolf. The wolf is being readied for release into the wild.

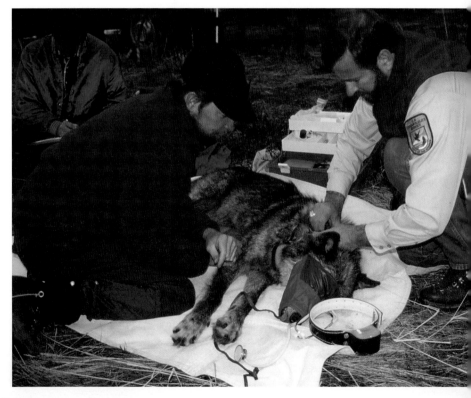

Biologists also use tag-and-release with birds. They place special nets, called mist nets, between trees. Birds fly into the nets and become stuck. The biologists remove the birds from the nets. Then they measure the birds and tag their legs or backs with small metal bands.

The bands' identification numbers help the biologists tell the birds apart. A telephone number may also be listed on each band. That way, if the bird is recaptured, the biologist conducting the study can be notified. Tag-and-release helps biologists record information about where birds travel and how long they live.

Eagles like this one can be tracked with leg bands.

Tracking Animals at Night

Just like with birds, biologists also use mist nets to catch bats. Since bats are most active at night, biologists attach glow sticks to their backs before they release them back into the wild. The glow sticks allow biologists to follow the bats back to their home. The sticks also allow biologists to follow the bats if they go hunting. The sticks only last a few hours. However, they provide a great source of light.

Another method for tracking animals at night uses black light. Once a small animal is caught, a fine powder is dusted all over its body. When the animal is released, the powder falls along the ground. This leaves a trail that can be followed using a special black light.

Amazingly, biologists have even found ways to track insects! They use the same instrument that other scientists use to forecast weather–Doppler radar. This radar allows biologists to find large groups of migrating insects. Thanks to radar tracking, farmers can be warned in time to protect their crops from hungry bugs.

Tracking is just one way biologists learn more about animals. Analyzing scat, examining habitats, and attaching collars to animals are all useful tracking methods. Biologists use these methods to collect important information. Animal tracking is a fascinating way to learn more about animals and the world around us!

Now Try This

Find Out About Wildlife Biologists

Have you ever wondered what it is like to be a wildlife biologist? With this activity, you'll be able to find out!

First, investigate what type of education is necessary. Use the Internet, your school library, and other sources to answer the following questions: How many years of study are required? What classes must students take to become wildlife biologists? Do they have to pass any special tests? What schools are considered the best for training students to become wildlife biologists? How has the job of being a wildlife biologist changed over the years?

After you have found out about the careers of some wildlife biologists, write a brief summary of them. In small groups, compare your summary with those of other classmates. Does being a wildlife biologist sound like an attractive career to you? Why or why not? Discuss these questions with your group.

Glossary

analyze *v.* to examine carefully and in detail.

biologists *n.* people who study living things.

classify *v.* to arrange in classes or groups; group according to some system.

data *n.* facts from which conclusions can be drawn; information.

hibernating *v.* spending the winter sleeping or in an inactive condition.

mammal *n.* any of a great many warm-blooded animals with a backbone and usually with hair.

measurement *n.* size or amount found by measuring.

migrate *v.* to go from one region to another with the change in the seasons.

scat *n.* animal droppings or waste.

tranquilizers *n.* drugs that relax or put animals to sleep.